Survival:

TOP Ideas To Survive EMP Attack + 20 Necessary Skills To Stay In-Touch With Your Family During The Disaster

Table of content:

Book 2

EMP Survival Guide

**How To Survive
An Electromagnetic Pulse Attack
and Prepare Yourself For Living
After The Power Grid Goes Down**

George Robbins

EMP Survival Guide:

How To Survive An Electromagnetic Pulse Attack and Prepare Yourself For Living After The Power Grid Goes Down

Introduction: What is it? And how was it Discovered?

The acronym "EMP" stands for "electromagnetic pulse". Traces of this electromagnetic pulse were first discovered with the detonation of high yield conventional weapons. But it wasn't until the first Atomic Bomb test in July of 1945 that the effects of a large EMP burst was seriously considered. Those who worked on the Manhattan Project for the then top secret U.S. atomic weapons program were duly informed of this possibility.

Further testing of high altitude nuclear explosions in the 1950's then confirmed what researchers had long suspected all along. And it was determined that the electromagnetic pulse of a strong enough nuclear grade weapon could potentially knock out the power grid of a substantially large region, potentially even an entire nation.

But not only would an EMP knock out the standard power structure it would also fry just about any electronic device within its reach! This means that in the immediate aftermath your car wouldn't start, your cell phone won't work, and all other electronic devices and appliances in your home would be completely fried and useless. This is how a frightening new possibility of warfare known as "EMP" had been discovered.

Chapter 1: Potential Weapon Applications of EMP

As damaging as EMP weapons can be to civil infrastructure, since they are generally non-lethal in nature, their application can be very tempting to state actors. These weapons allow for a significant disruption of an enemy's capabilities without the moral baggage of being responsible for massive civilian casualties. But a truly nefarious nation could potentially use these EMP weapons in a variety of ways to *maximize casualties and destruction*. This chapter explores all of the possible applications of weapons grade EMP.

Electro Magnetic Pulse Generator

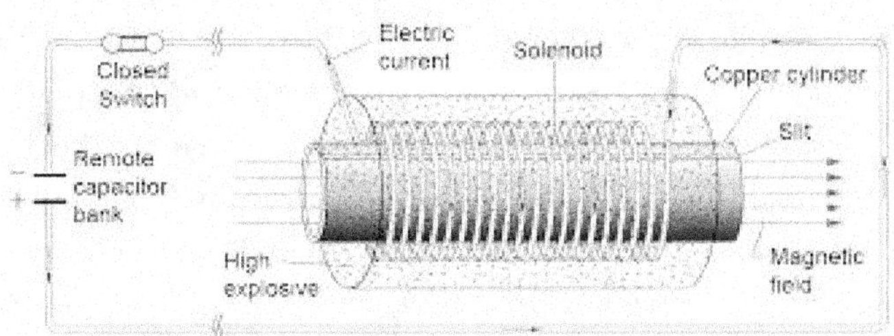

Electro magnetic pulse generators are still in development but if completed these highly focused, powerful weapons could potentially utilize microwave energy to create a massive and narrowly focused pulse that would be devastating both on the battle field and in the civilian theatre.

Tested with devastating success, "HEMP" refers to an instance of detonating a powerful nuclear weapon high in the atmosphere, in order to send out intense electro magnetic fields over a wide area of land below. The electromagnetic pulse created from just one instance of HEMP would be enough to fry almost all of the electronics in a large area. The wave of this pulse could potentially take out radio towers, and most power lines and cables. A HEMP weapon would also interact directly with the Earth's magnetic field, and utilize gamma rays to increase the power of the electromagnetic pulse.

<u>*Nemp*</u>

Nuclear electro magnetic pulse weapons are the standard weapons application of EMP that occurs as a direct result of a regular nuclear bomb blast. This is the general side effect of any nuclear blast but is particularly classified as such when it is intentionally use in this fashion.

<u>E-Bombs</u>

So called "E-Bombs" are highly efficient non-nuclear bombs that can unleash an intense magnetic field. These highly specialized weapons could be potentially produced so small that they could be fitted inside a suitcase. It is said that these weapons may be highly effective on the battlefield against specific military targets but would not pose that much of a threat to larger civilian infrastructure.

<u>High Power Microwave Weapons</u>

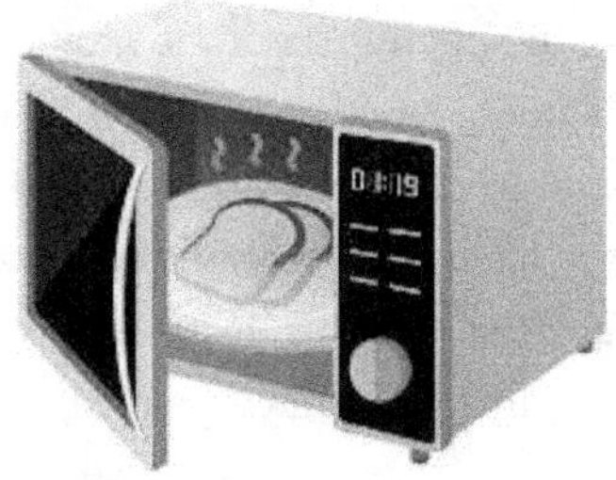

Described by the wavelength of their electromagnetic power, microwaves are used for a wide variety of applications from everything from radar to the microwave oven in your office that pops your popcorn. But HPM's or "high power microwaves" are on a whole other scale when it comes to the level of energy that is being produced.

In recent years many strides have been made to focus these HPM's into an EMP inducing weapon. By using something called a "flux compressor" these High Power Microwave Weapons can produce an incredibly formidable electromagnetic pulse that could wipe out any electrical equipment in its path. Even traditionally hardened and shielded devices are still affected by the penetrating wavelengths of High Power Microwave Weapons.

Remember when your mom told you not to stand in front of the microwave? Well there is a reason for that, because microwaves are able to permeate just about every surface, but unlike your relatively harmless microwave oven, a powerful HPM could wreak untold havoc.

Chapter 2: Ground Zero of an EMP

The ground zero of an EMP attack is certainly quite different from the ground zero of a nuclear or even conventional explosion. You won't find buildings shelled to their foundation or dead bodies smoldering in the street. The effects of an EMP are invisible and they only affect machinery, *not biological material* such as human beings consist of! In this chapter we will guide you through just what you might expect to find at the epicenter; *ground zero of an EMP attack!*

Strange Silence and Lights Out

The calm quiet of the aftermath of an EMP burst is one of the first standout features of such an attack. Imagine sitting down in your living room during a typical afternoon with TV blaring the news, dishwasher whirring through the latest round of dishes, your kids blaring music down the hall, and your next door neighbor cutting grass with the roar of a lawn mower. But in a split second, suddenly everything stops, no more TV, no more dishwasher, no more music, and even the lawnmower; inexplicably go quiet.

At first you think there must have been a local power outage; a simple enough explanation right? You instinctively reach for your phone to dial up your local power company, but you find the screen blank and lifeless.

You stare in disbelief thinking, "Didn't I just charge my phone? What is going on here?" Unable to call out for help you decide to take a step outdoors. But as you step outside and greet your neighbor whose *gas powered* lawn mower strangely conked out right when your power went out, the two of you turn to see another neighbor's car slowly skidding to a halt at the end of the street.

Another odd coincidence but you shrug it off as inopportune car trouble. You then see another neighbor futilely attempting to start his own car, putting in his key and cranking the ignition, but nothing but silence. Soon enough you would find that this silence in the aftermath of an EMP attack is permeating your entire neighborhood and the entirety of the ground zero of the electro magnetic pulse that has been unleashed. If the EMP burst occurred in the middle of the night the effect would be even more dramatic because all of your lighting would go out.

Even more disturbing, you would find that the trusty flashlight app on your phone is useless because all of your cell phones are fried! And even if you manage to fish out an old fashioned standalone "flashlight" (remember those?), you would be greatly distressed to find that even this simple instrument of illumination wouldn't work either! Your classic flashlight and the additional pair of batteries you stashed away, would be completely useless.

This is just how pervasive the electromagnetic pulse is, although you as a biological human being do not feel the pulse, in a split second it has flashed through every single piece of equipment you own. Sitting in the dark, you and your family will quickly realize that the only source of lighting available to you would be an old fashioned candle. In the aftermath of an EMP many will be wandering through their blackened neighborhoods with makeshift lanterns looking like they came straight out of the 1800's. This is the strange new world that is the ground zero of an EMP.

Spoiled Food

Besides the loss of our electronic devices, communication, and being able to travel freely down the road, the next biggest struggle will come from our refrigerator. Being left without power for days on end will obviously cause a massive spoilage of food. Knowing as much—in the immediate aftermath of an EMP attack—you should rank all of your food from the "most perishable" to the "least perishable".

You should then make it a priority to eat the most perishable items first. This means that for all of your food that you know will not last more than a couple of days unrefrigerated, you should eat as much of it as possible, you could even be a bit altruistic and share some of your food with your neighbors.

It's going to go bad anyway so you might as well create some good rapport with your neighbors. The least perishable food such as crackers, canned goods, and dried pasta, should be saved for the long haul, since this is food that you can rely upon in the intervening weeks without fear of it spoiling.

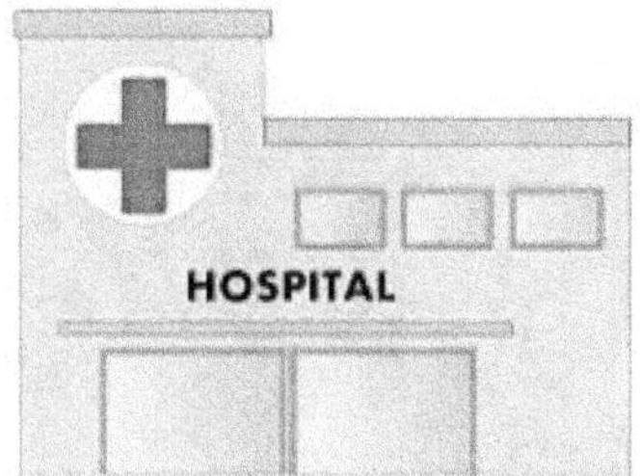

Even though an EMP blast would not directly kill anyone on the ground, the after affects could lead to significant casualties. And the most vulnerable of our population—those being cared for in our hospitals—would face the most dire of consequences. If an EMP successfully knocks out all power to the local grids, even generators wouldn't work and hospitals would truly be in the dark.

Patients in critical condition hooked up to life support would be the first to perish, flat lining as the machines that help keep them breathing go offline. After these patients perish, the next in line are those that are not necessarily hooked up to life support apparatus but who need certain life giving therapies and treatments that the power blackout would deprive them of.

After a few days these patients would die as well. One of the most disturbing aspects of an EMP is the high level of dead that it would leave in one of the most vulnerable segments of our population; those suffering from medical conditions. As you can see, such a dastardly attack would indeed bring about massive incidents of distress in our hospital system.

Social Chaos

Complete social breakdown would be the biggest fear of those trying to keep the peace in the aftermath of an EMP. With food spoiled, neighborhoods completely blacked out, and with no transportation to flee, citizens will feel cornered, and the propensity of civil unrest will be extraordinarily great.

How do you control a population that is on the brink of starvation, suffering a wide variety of medical illnesses, and with no solution in sight have lost all faith in government? It would be a difficult task for any leader to rein in such social chaos. And in such a tragic situation, a nation's own members could become the greatest threat of them all.

Chapter 3: Is EMP a Real Threat? And By Whom?

North Korea has been threatening to "incinerate" the United States for several years now. And now that the U.S. has a President that seems to fight fire *with fire*, even going so far as to state to the United Nations that if the U.S. is provoked, North Korea will be "destroyed", the threat from N.K. seems to loom largest. But North Korea is certainly not the only country that could surprise Western Civilization by turning the lights off with an EMP blast. There are several actors that could carry out such an attack. In this chapter we will outline some of the more plausible of these nightmare scenarios.

Many have joked and poked fun at those who bring up any concern in regard to tensions between the United States and the former Soviet Union. But although the Cold War is long over, and we live in a very different world, the fact still remains that the United States and Russia are the two most powerful militaries on the planet and even if these two nations are the best of friends today (contrary to what most policy wonks believe) it wouldn't take much for this relationship to deteriorate.

And having that said, Russia—of all nations—is rumored to have perhaps the most advanced EMP program in existence. So if push came to shove, there can be no doubt that the Kremlin has contingency plans of its own to use EMP against the United States. If Russia believed that a nuclear showdown with the United States was imminent for example, the prevailing theory is that Russian leadership would attempt to bypass the consequence of "mutually assured destruction" by launching such a devastating EMP that the U.S. would be knocked out before it could launch a single nuclear missile.

For such a thing to occur, the Russians would indeed have to have a powerful *and very precise* EMP weapon, and they would have to have a great deal of luck to create such a perfect electro magnetic storm that the U.S. is blacked out from coast to coast (they would also have to hope that U.S. nuclear subs wouldn't be able to reach them before being disabled by the pulse). Such unlucky odds for America may seem far fetched, but even the slightest chance of such a negative result needs to be taken into account.

Chinese Retaliatory Strike

Even in the best of times the United States and China have a rather tenuous relationship. There are quite a few ways that the U.S. and China can rub each other the wrong way and spark a devastating military conflict. For one thing—and as you can see is a common theme in this book—China is loosely allied with North Korea, and in light of the recent threats being leveled by North Korea to the United States, a conflict could erupt that pulls China right along with it.

Just how would such a nightmare scenario occur? Quite easily with the current stance that leader Kim Jong Un of Korea has been taking. Mr. Kim has been persistently pushing the limits of what the United States and the rest of the world can take. The world community is quickly discovering that if they tell Mr. Kim not to do something, in petulant defiance he will do it anyway. He was told not to launch missiles into the Sea of Japan, so he launches two missiles in rapid succession the next day.

And then after making threatening insinuations about attacking the U.S. military outpost of Guam in the middle of the Pacific Ocean, Mr. Kim was sternly warned to "not even think about it". So what does Mr. Kim do? The next day he informs the world media that he won't directly hit Guam—oh no, that would be crazy—but he would like to just set off a huge nuclear bomb right off the coastline instead!

The boyish leader of North Korea is literally testing the waters, pushing and pushing, inch by inch, to see just how far he can take things.

If North Korea did drop a nuclear bomb off the shore of Guam, while it may not lead to direct casualties, obviously the United States could not (without completely losing face and all credibility) stand by and let North Korea get away with blowing up nuclear bombs just outside their harbor! If the U.S. allowed this they would have to allow anything. Then again—if the U.S. does respond to this severe provocation, the crafty North Korean leader could rightfully proclaim that their nuclear test off the shores of Guam didn't technically hurt anyone.

Most would see the flaws in this logic and call this nonsense out for what it was, but push come to shove, China may decide to back its traditional ally. In this scenario, North Korea pushes its luck, takes things way to far, bombs the coast of Guam and forces the U.S. to strike North Korea. China alarmed that its neighbor is being incinerated, and fearing what might happen next, takes the initiative and drops a massive EMP over the U.S. in order to freeze the U.S. assault in its tracks. Let's hope none of this nightmare scenario ever occurs.

<u>North Korea Makes Good on its Threats</u>

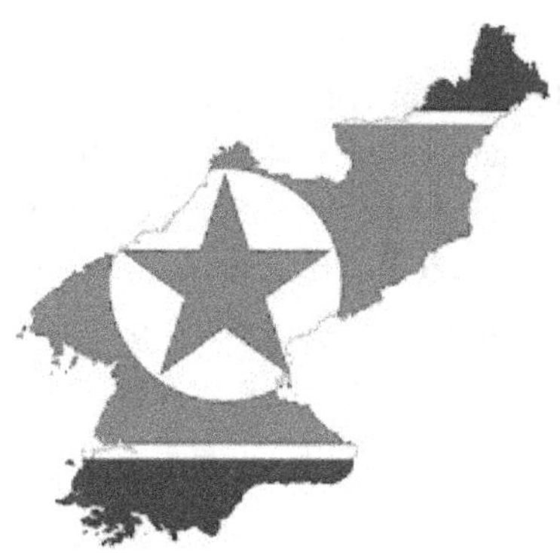

No one quite knows what Kim Jong Un (or as some have dubbed him; the "rocket man") is up to when it comes to his ambitious nuclear missile program. Many have made the claim that the North Korean leader only wishes to have a nuclear deterrent as a safeguard and collateral against any future U.S. attempt at regime change. This argument contends that while non-nuclear countries such as Iraq and Libya have faced grueling regime change either directly or tacitly backed by the United States, nations with nuclear weapons remain safe from such intrusions.

Directly feeding into this belief more than anything else is the glaring fact that the long time dictator of Libya, Momar Kaddafi actually voluntarily turned over his weapons of mass destruction, including the components of a nascent nuclear program with the promise from the Bush administration to never interfere with the Libyan government. But it only took a change of administration a few years later to have President Obama leading the charge to run Kaddafi out of power during the Arab Spring.

If Kaddafi had a nuclear bomb to play as his trump card, this probably never would have happened. It seems that Kim Jong Un has paid attention to this example of a head of state cooperating with nuclear disarmament only to perish, and taken the lesson to heart. This is why for many, it seems that Kim is primarily bluff and bluster, using his nuclear weapons to deter the United States, but would never be crazy enough to actually use them.

But then again, there are many who would point out that if all Kim sought was a nuclear deterrent, all he really needed was one nuclear bomb, just one nuclear weapon is usually enough to deter an outright land invasion of a country, yet Kim kept going after that *one bomb*, he kept going after *two bombs*, and he kept going at *20 bombs*. North Korea is now producing nuclear weapons—and ever more powerful and stronger grade nuclear weapons—at such an exponential rate, that some policy analysts are beginning to sound the alarm that a simple nuclear deterrent is not the only thing Kim is seeking.

For them it seems that Kim is attempting something else entirely. Kim Jong Un seems to have three goals in mind with his nuclear build up; either bully or destroy South Korea and unify the entire Korean peninsula under his reign, get revenge on Japan for the atrocities Japan committed against them during World War Two, and perhaps, just perhaps drop a massive EMP on the United States to make it unable to respond (at least in a timely manner) to North Koreas attacks on its neighbors.

According to this dreadful theory, North Korea would take out the U.S. electrical grid first with a powerful EMP, then bomb, and or flood troops into South Korea, while simultaneously decimating Japan with nuclear and or conventional weapons, hoping that the U.S. would be literally "powerless" to stop them. It is for a scary scenario like this that the U.S. needs to make sure that it can either prevent, or mostly withstand an EMP attack intact, so that North Korea would not be able to make good on its threats.

President Barack Obama made a deal with Iran to delay their nuclear program for 10 years, but many skeptical observers believe that Iran is probably continuing their development regardless. Coincidentally enough Iran already has long rage missiles courtesy of North Korea. The fact that North Korea has exported military hardware to Iran is what led President George Bush to make North Korea and Iran, part of what he termed the, "Axis of Evil".

On the surface, the two nations of North Korea and Iran do not have much in common. North Korea is a communist nation that eschews religion while Iran is a hardcore religious state. But despite their diametrically opposed belief systems, both nations have an equal sense of antagonism when it comes to the United States. And this is precisely why the American CIA under the Bush administration had such fear of these two nations actively collaborating with each other.

If Iran secretly produced a bomb, or if North Korea actually colluded with Iran enough to ship them an already constructed weapon, Iran could produce an unpleasant surprise in the form of an EMP burst over the middle of the United States. It would be with terrible irony that the so-called axis of evil would finally live up to all the hype and the fear mongering, by creating an electro magnetic variant of former President Bush's smoking gun.

Terrorists Deploy Suitcase EMP

So far in this chapter we have discussed the dangers of other nations subjecting the United States to a nationwide power failure through an EMP attack. Now lets explore the unpleasant possibility of terrorists using a much smaller, so-called "Suitcase EMP" to specifically knock out the power grid of a targeted city. In this scenario a small band of terrorists could unload a suitcase EMP in the middle of downtown New York creating a city-wide blackout.

Not only that, since the infrastructure was so thoroughly fried the terrorists are fully aware that it will take months for city officials to get the power back on. In such an attack, the black out itself would no doubt simply be the first step of the plan, and after the power grid is shut down, the terrorists would then move on to stage to which would be subjecting the disabled city to horrific terrorist attacks through conventional bombings, mass shootings, and even stabbings.

It's an awful thing to think about, but even a small suitcase EMP could lead to such horrible consequences. In order to exact such damage, it is believed that the total cost to finance such a mission—including the gathering of all technical components of the device—would cost less than a couple thousand dollars. A truly sobering statistic, and yet another reason analysts are staying up at night in the never ending struggle to keep the rest of us safe.

Chapter 4: What Defense is there from EMP?

The effects of an EMP are projected to be absolutely devastating to national infrastructure. So the question naturally arises; is there any way to protect against or prevent an EMP strike? As the protectors of a nation, institutions like the United States Pentagon have spent countless hours exploring every possible contingency plan to keep their country out of harms way. And when it comes to an EMP attack, many different contingencies for defense and preservation of the nation have been explored.

But it isn't just those on the national level that should carry the entire burden, each and every one of us as citizens should also be educated as much as possible on the means of our own survival. Having that said, this chapter uses a dual approach describing how the government as well as the individual citizen may be able to defend against the onslaught of an EMP.

Metallic Shielding

In order to use metallic shielding on electrical equipment, you will need to use a continuous piece of shielding such as copper or steel would provide. These metal shields usually don't completely cover the interior however, and will most likely consist of some exceedingly small holes for ventilation. Additional, auxiliary materials are usually used in order to compensate for this perceived gap in security. The shielding should be about half a millimeter thick in order to provide the best protection from the blast of an electromagnetic pulse.

Tailored Hardening

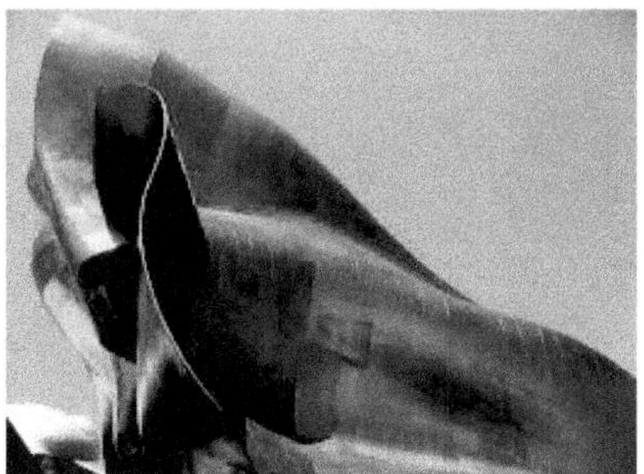

When it comes to tailor made hardening of electrical equipment in defense of a potential EMP attack, the first thing that needs to be considered is whether or not the system itself will be viable if hardening is achieved. With tailor hardening you are only encasing the most sensitive pieces of the electronics in metal cases. Being able to differentiate what part of an appliance or device needs hardening and what parts could do without is crucial in keeping an EMP defense within budget. But although this method is cheaper it has not proven to be quite as reliable as complete metallic shielding.

Preparing the Private Sector

Many have attempted to claim that there is not contingency plan when it comes to private sector infrastructure. This couldn't be further from the truth. Since civil infrastructure of the private sector could be severely damaged, measures have been taken to put into place powerful surge protectors that could not only withstand a bolt of lighting, but could also take on an electromagnetic pulse. This is a step in the right direction, but these surge protectors are by no means full proof and could easily be overwhelmed, but it is at least a start when it comes to preparing the private sector.

Detecting and Knocking out An EMP Device

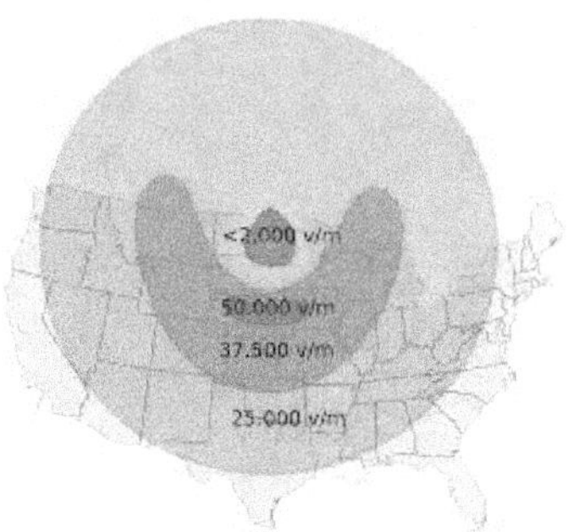

In recent years, primarily due to provocations from North Korea, the U.S. has stepped up its efforts to perfect methods of shooting down nuclear missiles and other offensive weapons, in mid flight. The conventional method is to use offensive missiles such as the "patriot" class interceptors to aim, shoot, and knock enemy missiles out of the sky. In addition to this, there are also projects in the works with laser technology to shoot down incoming objects.

The U.S. military has prototypes of ground laser batteries as well as continued research into space based laser platforms as was touted in Ronald Reagan's "Strategic Defense Initiative" program of the 1980's. And when it comes to something more subtle such as a suitcase EMP that terrorists are attempting to deploy in the middle of a city, man's best friend may be his dog after all.

There are several programs that have successfully trained the miraculous nose of the common dog to find and ferret out the components of what would make up an EMP device. So whether its through a patriot missile, a ground based laser, Ronald Reagan's SDI, or your dog's trusty sniffer, there are ways to detect and potentially knock out an EMP device.

Chapter 5: Important Food and Medical Supplies

Although there is not much the individual citizen can do if their power grid is knocked down—to turn the power back on—there are several other life saving aspects you can thoroughly prepare for. First and foremost on your list of preparation for an EMP attack would be adequate food and medical supplies.

Due to the nature of the crisis, these supplies would have to be completely nonperishable items that you could leave out in the item or packed away in boxes without any damage to the contents of the supplies. In this chapter we will explore some of the best of these nonperishable food and medical supplies to have on hand in the event of an EMP blast.

<u>*First Aid Kit*</u>

This is prepping 101 for just about any disaster, but yes, in the event of an EMP the traditional First Aid Kit would be a tremendous resource to have available. You should have a fully stocked kit with such medical supply staples such as cold packs, hydrogen peroxide, some Tylenol, and most importantly, needle, thread, and scissors. The latter items are of extreme import if you have to sow your own stitches. It may not always be pretty, but basic supplies like these will help you to survive the aftermath of an EMP blast.

Garlic

This herb is good to eat and heal your wounds at the same time! You probably recognize Garlic more for its use as a seasoning, but if you were to sprinkle a little bit of it in your wounds, it would work to greatly ease your pain and speed up the healing process. Garlic has special compounds that help to promote blood clotting and promote the formation of new platelets at the sight of the injury helping it to scab over and heal much faster than it would otherwise. So be sure to pack some garlic!

The aftermath of an EMP can be a hazardous place, especially at night when it is difficult to see. These extra risk factors could lead to all kinds of injuries. This is why having a good roll of gauze on hand is critical to offset the danger. Immediately after you get injured wrap up the injury up with gauze and allow the area to pressurize in place so that it can heal. Gauze is an important medical supply to have.

Canned Goods

Some of the best food you could ever have stashed away in your cupboards are canned goods. These cans of food can last for decades. So yes, even though you may have laughed at your crazy uncle who kept a large supply of emergency canned goods big enough to fill a walk in closet, in our uncertain world such a practice is completely reasonable. In the face of an EMP attack when food might become incredibly scarce, such things don't seem quite so ridiculous! So yes, stock up on your canned goods!

<u>*Save Some Beef Jerky*</u>

Beef Jerky and other dried out meat are not just a good snack; they are a marvelous lifeline of protein preservation! Beyond beef jerky, just about any meat can be dried out with the right combination of salty brine, and through established drying techniques. If you don't know how to do it yourself, you can always purchase a nice supply of already dried beef and otherwise jerky! It's a great foodstuff to help see you through the worst of an EMP!

Conclusion: Surviving an Electro Magnetic Pulse

It is definitely a scary thing to wake up and find your entire city block out of power. It is horrifying then to find that you can't even start your car to flee the scene! But these are the startling realities of an EMP attack. In the chance that some rogue actor decides to implement such a devious strike against us, we have to be vigilant and we have to be prepared. I hope this book has left you just a little bit more informed, and more importantly reassured, of how you can survive an electromagnetic pulse. Thank you for reading!

S H A R O N   R E E V E S

20 Best Survival Skills To Stay In-Touch With Your Family During The Disaster

Survival
Communication

Survival Communication:

20 Best Survival Skills To Stay In-Touch With

Your Family During The Disaster

Introduction

Emergency communication must be one of your top priorities in an emergency disaster scenario. The ability to receive or to send information could mean the difference between you and your loved ones surviving or not.

Many of us do not realize this fact, but whenever you transmit a message through any device that is connected to the communication infrastructure, you are taking an inherent risk.

There are thousands of hackers in the United States alone working all day to steal as much data as they possibly can, ranging from a single hacker in the basement to well organized criminal groups.

Each time you use a modern form of communication, whether it be your smart phone, your tablet, your laptop, your email, the internet, or even social media, there is a perfectly good chance that at some point your information will become compromised.

Even though some of the communication methods we will discuss in this chapter rely on electricity, they do not rely on phone networks that the internet and phone companies provide to you.

It has been proven, time after time, that our modern communication infrastructure is extremely vulnerable to even the smallest or shortest of disasters.

Cell networks become overwhelmed, cell towers are taken offline, and so on.
The simple fact of the matter is that our communication infrastructure is not designed to handle emergencies.

And yet the vast majority of Americans living today are incredibly reliant on their mobile devices. They don't realize just how ineffective these devices are going to be during a disaster.

Widespread damage to cellular infrastructure was inflicted in the summer of 2012 as storms swept through the mid-Atlantic alone, and a larger scale catastrophe means that the entire country could be affected.

When these disasters take place, people will be unable to use their phones to access the internet or to call for help through 911.

Chapter 1. Prepare a Survival Communication Plan In Advance

It is vital to make sure that your whole family is ready and conversant within the event of a disaster or emergency. You cannot always be along with them when these events happen therefore you should have plans to face such kind of disasters and emergencies. Also make sure that you're able to contact and find each other. Don't forget your pets in whole of the situation. They will be more worried than you. Here is how you can get mentally equipped for such an unfortunate event;

Prepare Yourself:

Before anyone else, prepare yourself to face any kind of disaster or emergency. Remember that you are going to survive the situation only if you are well planned and ready ahead of the event. There are certain steps that you can take in such a situation. Let's have a look;

Before a Disaster:

According to the American Red Cross, you must be taking the following steps in any of such events; Have a meeting with your family and household members.

Discuss and decide the type of disasters and emergencies you are expecting to face in such a situation.

Get prepared accordingly.

Assign responsibilities among all the available members.

If any of the family members is in army then decide how you will carry out things if he or she gets deployed.

During the Disaster:

If you get separated: You can get separated from your family members and friends and fellows during a disaster. This happens very commonly.

Here is what you should do if you get separated from the closed ones during a state of emergency: • Decide two places to meet, for instance, • Exactly outside your home in case of a fire.

• Outside your neighborhood if you are unable to return to your home or have been asked to evacuate.

• Select a person to contact who resides outside the area of disaster.

You can text or call him from your mobile phone or through internet if the local phone lines have gotten out of service or are overloaded. It is important to keep emergency contact information saved in your phone or written in a diary.

• If you are asked to evacuate: You can also be asked to evacuate in the cases of emergencies and disasters. In that case, take the following steps; • Select the place where you would go in such a situation.

Also decide the route through which you will reach at your safe haven. You can choose a motel or you can decide to stay with your friends or some family members living outside the area of the disaster. You can also opt for an evacuation shelter in case you don't find any other place to go instantly.

It may sound crazy but practice to evacuate. Yes! Practice to evacuate your home at least twice a year. After evacuation, drive to your destination through a specified route. Also mark other alternative routes on your map to reach the destination in case the original or the shortest one is impassable.

Also plan for your pets. Keep a list ready of the pet friendly hotels or rest houses or animal shelters or any living place which is ready to welcome your pets along with you on your evacuation route.

Inform your family and friends about your safe arrival at the destination.

Satellite Phone

Even if the phone networks collapse, a satellite phone will still work flawlessly. The reason why is because satellite phones do not use the networks that normal phones do.

How satellite phones work instead is they bounce a signal to a satellite before connecting to the device that you want to talk to.

Satellite phones are therefore great for two kinds of disasters:

1.   A Wilderness Survival Situation
2.   A Large Scale Urban Disaster

Granted, satellite phones are quite expensive, but they will also be a very wise investment because you can maintain contact with your friends, relatives, and the outside world even if the cell service towers are no longer working.

Chapter 2.Best Survival Radios

Walkie-Talkie

We should all be familiar with this one. The walkie-talkie, also known as the two-way radio, is an excellent way for you to maintain verbal communication with others (though within a limited range), because it uses a non-phone network.

While the range of walkie-talkie vary by the model, most can allow you to communicate with people from thirty-five up to fifty miles.

Walkie-talkies are also dirt cheap, easily accessible, easy to store and carry, use a wide number of channels, and have a long battery life.

A large variety of different types of walkie-talkie set with wild features are available in your local market. Here we are discussing types of walkie-talkies in respect to their features;

Walkie-talkie with Far Reaching Transmission.

Not all details provided in the manuals of the walkie-talkie sets are right in their origin. Therefore, don't believe instantly on all of the information written in the sales literature when selecting a set for your disaster kit. The reason is that the distance calculated by the manufacturers is usually measured in an area with vacuum and sound travels faster and farther in vacuum. But in an area with buildings, trees, traffics and other interferences it is not possible for you to achieve the exact results. Two types of radios can help in this scenario. One is FRS *i.e.* Family Radio Service and the other is GMRS *i.e.* General Mobile Radio Service.

Walkie-talkie with Multiple Radio Channels.

Multiple radio channels are usually available in cities. Many are allotted to different areas already. Similarly, a business might have allotted different radio channels for different business functions. Whatever the case is, decide how many channels you want your radio to have especially when you intend to add in your preparedness for a disaster kit. It is crucial. Most of the walkie-talkies are either FRS or GMRS that shows that use multiple channels, for instance, GMRC uses channels from number 15 to 22.

An important point to remember is that many walkie-talkie sets also offer privacy codes. These codes can block you outside chatter on a specific channel. Further remember that the calls are not private and anyone can listen to them. the only privacy you get is that your calls cannot be interrupted by anyone.

Walkie-talkies with Batteries.

Walkie-talkie run on batteries as this feature makes them portable. It is important to know the kind of batteries that the new addition in your disaster kit is going to need for power supply. These radios come with a large variety of power supply options. Some of them use AA or AAA regular alkaline batteries that are disposable while others might be using rechargeable batteries. Remember that in a disaster, there might be no electricity supply available for you to charge your Walkie-talkie sets and once, the rechargeable battery is out, you will be out as well. Therefore, buy walkie-talkie sets with disposable batteries and also stock such batteries in your emergency kit so you don't run out of power supply anytime during the disaster. Also don't install batteries in your set while it is just kept placed in your kit because batteries automatically drain on being kept in the device for too long.

Good warranty, compatibility of the set with other devices and the handiness of the users must also be kept in mind along with the number of supported channels, distance coverage and type of power supply sources while buying walkie-talkie radios for your emergency kit. Technology evolves everyday therefore also check for new available options too.

CB Radios

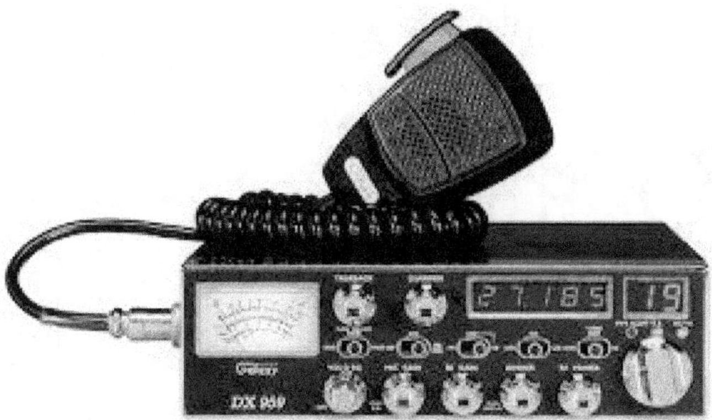

CB radios are most commonly used today by truckers, and will be a reasonable choice for a catastrophe scenario.

The biggest limitation to the CB radio is its limited range (generally no more than ten to fifteen miles). Therefore, it is only a short-range communication device and must be treated as such, but it will still work even if your smart or cell phone does not.

We will talk about CB radios in greater depth and the various codes there are for them later in this book when we talk about the best radios for you to own for survival.

Ham Radio

The ham radio is widely favored by many survivalists and with good reason. Military, law enforcement, and search-and-rescue teams also widely utilize the ham radio because of the fact that it can be used even when cell phones cannot and they have a wide range.

Ham radios also feature a scanner that will allow you to keep yourself up-to-date on what's happening in your area.

You do need a license to get a ham radio, and we'll discuss how to acquire this license later in this book. Along with that, we'll discuss ham radios in greater depth too.

<u>**Army Radio**</u>

If Walkie-talkies are no longer available, then you might have access to a much lesser used technology amongst civilians. I remember fondly the time that my father showed me his military issued radio and this thing was massive. We're talking about a big green box with an antenna that was twice the height of my body when I was seven years old. The beauty is that this type of technology is no longer only held by the military and you can go to a "military shop" to purchase one. This type of shop isn't particularly called a military shop but it is where you can buy semi-automatic weapons, camo, and other "military" gear. These radios are a bit unwieldy to say the least but perhaps that's what makes them durable. You will need to read the user manual for this.

Amateur Radio

You can get licensed to operate your own HAM radio and there is a clear distinction between regular radio and a Home Amateur Radio. Depending on your level of clearance, you can get anywhere from communicating with boats on the sea and other HAM radio operators to military personnel and helicopters. Needless to say, if you were trying to use this to communicate with loved ones then they would need to be certified anyway.

Citizens Band Radio

However, that isn't the only type of radio that's out there and this means you can target something that's normally referred to as CB radio, which is a long-distance radio channel meant for citizens. This is the type of radio that's often utilized by truckers and the police. Please understand that CB radio only has a mile radius of up to 100 miles at maximum, so you are not likely going to be able to contact people who are far off. Just so you know, the most common place to mount this device is inside of your car (hence the popularity with truckers and drivers) because you can usually keep in constant contact with anyone in your city. Most cities don't even span the total of 50 miles, so you are likely going to be able to contact anyone you need to in the city that you live in and considering most cities are nowhere near 100 miles of each other, you will find it is handy for emergency contacts inside of your car if you get stuck on a backroad of some sort. I'm honestly surprised that this don't come standard issue with our cars... we might not have so many horror movies.

Additionally, if you're a boat operator then you might also know about the MB radio or Marine Band radio, meant for anyone travelling on the open waters. This is extremely useful for most boats out at low waters of the sea. This is a short-range radio (most of the time) and is good for many things, such as when you get lost or asking other fishermen where good fishing holes are for the day. Having said that, all the previous radios mentioned in this chapter require that you both have one so it's important that you both go down that road together or else it will be next to useless unless you can find someone nearby that will be able to receive and relay your messages.

GMRS Radios

GMRS radios are a good choice for communication in a survival situation for a number of reasons:

- They are more popular than CB radios
- Easy to use/user friendly
- Cheap and easy to get
- Do not require an FCC license

That being said, GMRS radios also have a number of limitations, especially in regard to their range and power. If you can tap into a repeater, however, then you will be able to increase your range by several hundred miles. Otherwise, your range is going to be pretty limited similar to a walkie-talkie.

Chapter 3. Flares

A flare permits you to contact others from long distances for help and are a clear sign that you are in trouble.

Flares are universally accepted as a signal of distress, so if you shoot a flare into the sky, anybody within your general area who sees it will come to your aid.

Smoke Signaling

Signaling for help with smoke is another great way to communicate with others, even if it is rather primitive.

The best way to create an effective and highly visible smoke is to select a clearing on the top or side of the hill. Burn green brush so white smoke is created that will be more visible.

You can also send specific messages with the aid of a blanket. What you need to do is soak your blanket in water so it will not burn. Then you throw your blanket over the fire until no more smoke is traveling upward.

You will then pull the blanket back to send a puff of white smoke into the air, and then throw it back over the fire.

Here are the universal signals and their meaning when communicating with smoke:

- One Puff: means there is no danger or need for alarm, but whoever you are signaling needs to stay on the lookout for future signals.

- Two Puffs: means everything is going smoothly and your camp has been safely established. All is well and it is safe to proceed.

- Three Puffs: means there is danger and cause for alarm; enemies may be approaching. Either come to aid or evacuate the area.

Alternatively, you can send an SOS message with smoke signaling. The universal SOS message is three short beats, three long beats, and then three short beats.

So in the case of smoke signaling, you would do three quick puffs rapidly together, three long puffs, and then three more quick rapid puffs.

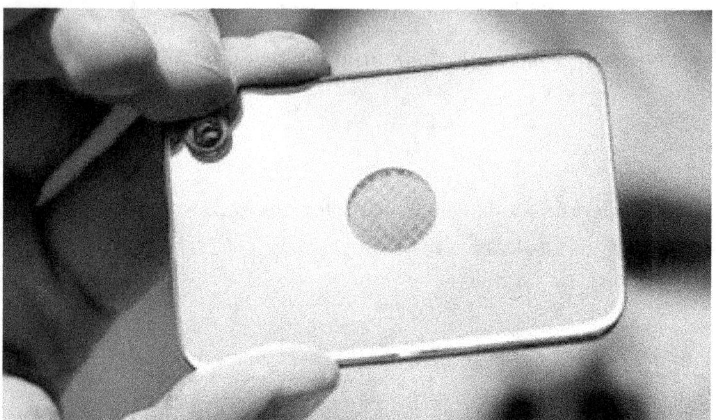

You can also communicate or request aid with a signal mirror. On a clear sunny day, you simply use your mirror to reflect the light of the sun and signal for help.

In the event that you lack a mirror, you can also use a beer or soda can and polish the bottom with chocolate to make it more reflective. You could also use the bottom reflective surface of a CD or DVD.

It's extremely easy to use a signaling mirror as well. Just follow these steps:

1.   Bring the mirror to your eye

2.   Make sure that the surface of the mirror is not obscured by your fingers or hat

3.   Tilt the mirror toward the sun

4.   You should now see a small beam of light

5.   Move the beam of light toward your target

Simple, right?

You can also send an SOS message with a signal mirror: three short light flashes, three long light flashes, and then three more short ones.

I put these in the same category because they kind of come after the Facebook or email option because of their purpose. Sure, nowadays we use Twitter to display rebellions and to get almost immediate access to information because of how small each tweet is but that doesn't mean that people think of Twitter or even Instagram first in terms of contacting their loved ones during an emergency and so that's why we've listed it in the slightly less obvious category. Needless to say, Google+ is also here due to the fact that almost no one actually uses Google+ anymore but it still exists as a Google feature.

<u>*Asking a Police Officer*</u>

As much as the news in the media like to portray police officers, police officers pretty much run the behind-the-scenes network when it comes to communication within an emergency. If you go to a police officer, that's not busy, they are likely to assist you in whatever way you need because you are a person who is seeking help from a police officer. It's not really their job to do this but most police officers will do things that are not necessarily required of them simply because they got into their job because they love helping people or they like the feeling of being needed. This means that if you ask them to get a message to your loved one then they would be able to use their resources to ensure that your message gets sent. It's slightly less obvious, but it's nowhere near as advanced as some of the things we'll discuss here.

Using a Pay Phone

At this point it's kind of like I'm talking about a dinosaur when I talk about a pay phone because most people hear the option of going and utilizing a pay phone and then they begin to question whether those devices even exist anymore or even what the device is, depending on how young that individual is. The truth is that they are a legal mandate by the city and so while they did remove a giant portion of public phones from cities around the United States of America, that doesn't mean that they removed the all. The truth of the matter is that you are more likely to find a payphone inside of downtown then you are if you're outside of downtown because downtown is where the most collected amount of individuals are that would be able to benefit from the use of a pay phone. You see, even though the pay phone is legally mandated they still put it in places where it makes sense to keep maintenance on the machine as low as possible.

Chapter 4. Light-Safe Signals

Here's another one for the individuals trying to communicate with the other individuals across the street. This type of technique involves you having a flashlight and the individual you're trying to contact having a flashlight. Essentially, all you want to do is you want to flash a light twice to see if they are alright and wait for the other person to flash once to say that they are okay. It takes the purpose of the conversation between two neighborhood houses and reduces it to the core reasons of why the two of you are conversing in the first place. However, that doesn't mean that you can't go any further than that because if you learn how to send out Morse code and you teach the other individual how to send out Morse code, the two of you can begin to talk to each other with flashlights without even needing a cell phone or a walkie-talkie because Morse code was the original form of long range electronic translation. Morse code isn't that difficult to implement either because you simply wait for the start of a sequence of blinks and non-blinks and then once that sequence is over, you write down either a word or a phrase or a character. Either way, once you rinse and repeat this action of few tens to hundreds of times, you are then able to connect it all together and read the entirety of the material in the safe place that is your home.

Google Voice Texting

There are some obscure parts of Google and this is important to understand because there are services like Google Voice and Google Hangouts. If your cell phone doesn't work but you can get in contact with Google Voice and if your cell phone is attached to a cellular plan, you can call people from Google Voice. You can also text them if you need to because Google Voice gives you the option of having a secondary number and the most common secondary number that they have for most people trying to use Google Voice is a Texas number. I keep Google Voice around for when the going gets tough, it's great to have a secondary plan where I can contact people with something other than my cellular device because it's not like people expect mail today.

That's not the only limitation that comes with Google Voice though because you also have the fact that if you do not have any cellular number attached to a cellular plan and you attempt to call an individual through Google Voice without having one, it will direct you to the default phone line and then you will be blocked. In some cases, you can actually mitigate this and get it to read as the Google Voice number in your account but you have to have a specific type of phone in order to achieve this. It's really just easier to make sure that you have a cellular plan attached to your phone in case of an emergency but it is useful in texting people because it doesn't deny you access to that if you don't have a cellular plan.

Google Hangouts

Google Hangouts is a software that has been around for quite a bit of time but didn't gain as much traction as Skype or SnapChat or any of the other video based messengers and this is because Google didn't really do a good job selling their software. That doesn't mean that it's going to be the most popular in the market but it does have one feature that's very useful in case of an emergency and I don't mean a 911 emergency but just contacting your relatives emergency. You see, if you decide that you want to set up a Google Voice account and get a number, that number will be registered to your Google Hangouts account. Once the number is registered to your Google Hangouts account, you can then begin to expect to be able to call individuals over Google Hangouts in the web browser and I find that this is very useful as a backup cell phone whenever I don't have a cellular plan and I make sure that all of my family members are aware that this number exists. Now I will say that this is kind of limited because if you trying to contact anyone that's outside of the US, it's going to cost you money but as long as you're calling people inside of America then you're usually going to have a phone call free of charge. This is because Google utilizes its own VoIP system in order to allow people to not only contact individuals over the phone but also contact individuals over the internet.

Send A Text Via "send-a-text" Technology

Google voice isn't the only place where you can send out text messages and this is very important to understand because there is a difference. Google Voice gives you a phone number and this phone number can be saved inside of the contacts list of your loved ones, which means that they won't block you or their service provider won't block you whenever you try to contact them. With that said, if you don't mind not having a recognizable phone number, then you can go with a secondary option if you prefer not set up a Google Voice account and that is to send text with websites that will send texts for you. Normally, you just type in the website and then type in the text along with where the phone number is and hit send in order to send out your text. This is actually a technology that's been around for almost a decade or two that a lot of people in the First World countries simply don't know about because why would you need to know about it if you have a cell phone plan in the first place. Certain job opportunities provide you with the ability to be in a country are there are no cell phones and this becomes extremely problematic whenever you need to send text messages and produce phone calls and the only thing that you have is the internet. Not only that, but the internet is watched. This is why it's very useful to have such technology that can provide you with the cellular services that you need on a connection that you didn't expect it.

Ironically, whenever most people say that they can't do the previous two, their reasoning is that they have no access to a computer and this is funny because of how wrong the thought processes are. Why would anyone buy a computer that they didn't test it first? This is a tested and tried rule when it comes to products. A customer doesn't care about what a giant list of hardware specifications say about the hardware but just that the hardware works in the way that they expected. In order to do that with computers, items that literally costs hundreds of dollars, most stores allow the computers being sold to be displayed on a shelf that can then be used. This means that the customer not only has access to a computer but, most of the time, because they primarily test for speed in the browser, they also have internet access on the computer so if you don't have a phone and don't even have a computer to utilize the tools I just gave you, you can actually go to one of these stores and use their computer for a quick second to utilize the tools I just gave you, but that doesn't mean that this doesn't come with limitations.

First of all, remember that the computer is not yours. You may be using the computer but the computer is not yours and so you have to be respectful of the company where the computer is stored at and you have to understand that some businesses do not connect it to the internet but most do.

Therefore, you are taking a risk at this point. However, in case of an emergency you can utilize this as a last-ditch effort to contact an individual that you may need assistance from. However, if you are so desperate that you need to go to the Walmart down the road so that you can use computers on their display, then I highly suggest you go talk to a police officer if you can. If the world is ending, don't expect the internet to be up for more than a few weeks. It takes a lot of manpower to keep the internet running.

Since we're on the aspect of utilizing desktops and laptops in order to send out messages, this springs up the instant messenger that people used to use and have on their desktops. You see, for every language that there is on the planet there's likely a chat system that can be geared specifically towards that language.

This means that if you give it enough time, you will eventually find any chat system that is specifically built for your language and your needs. You have to realize that before people had text messaging on their phones, they had instant messenger via AOL or some other service on their desktop. This means that they have had more time to develop software packages for desktop instant messengers than they have had cell phones.

Needless to say, you will need to have the other individual sign up to this beforehand but it is a good option to have these types of technologies available on hand if you just so happen to get into a binding spot where you need to use these to contact whoever you're trying to contact over to the other side.

Chapter 5. Online Chat Rooms

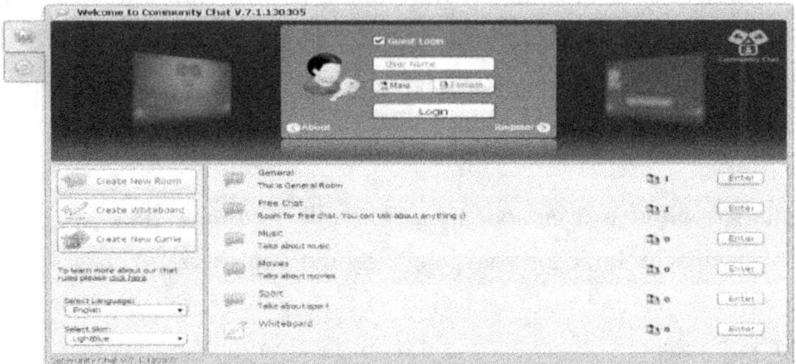

Another Advanced option is a command line trap room. You do have online websites where you can just go in and randomly chat with a user but there are still command line chat rooms and the reason why this is a more advanced version is because this is usually referred to as a relay chat. A relay chat takes identified nodes on a network and connect them so that they relay messages to each other, which is why it was one of the very first methods of creating a chat system. You can use someone else's relay chat system and set this up on everyone's computer or you can create your own with some digging in a little research, but the honest truth is that an online relay chat room is capable of working on any device that receives a internet connection.

As odd as it may seem, landline phones are still in use and a lot of people find it rather on that one of the main advices for people is to get a landline phone in case of an emergency because they don't understand why you would need such a device if you have a cell phone. However, you have to realize that the landline phone was built to withstand some incredible stuff and it was also built in a very unique way. If you truly have a landline phone and not something that requires auxiliary power but the landline phone that just accepts the phone line, you will be able to run that phone whenever the power is out because the power that the landline phone receives comes from the phone line itself. This is incredibly ingenious but also something that many people seem to forget whenever they go to buy their smartphone and don't see a landline phone as something being needed.

The Spark Gap Transmitter:

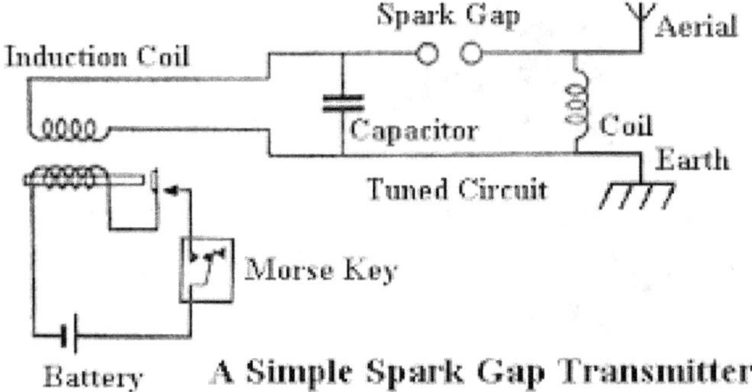

A Simple Spark Gap Transmitter

The spark gap transmitters were first used in 1800 and literally the first device to be used for radio transmission. These transmitters work by generating spark across a spark gap in the transmitter. Their advantage is that they are easily manufactured and are easily used. They have a huge range working over a number of frequencies and also as a back-up for distress messages on the international distress frequency of 500 kHz (600 meters) right up to the beginning of World War II.

The thing make its use is illegal, is its range. Also transmission of signals and understanding them require expertise as the messages transmitted can only be understood if the person knows the Morse code or they have their own transmission code to interpret what is being said.

Repeaters:

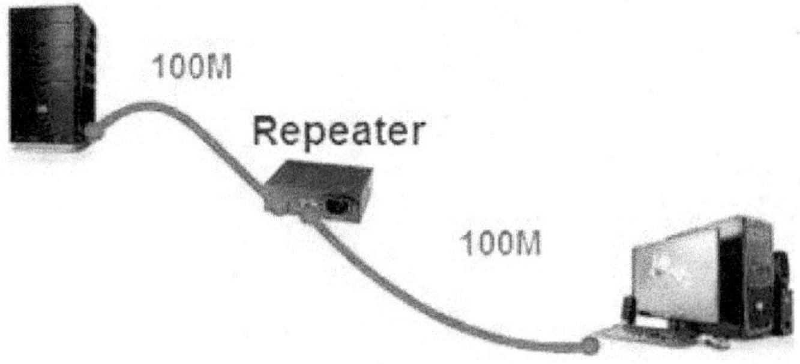

A repeater is a device which can transmit signals repeatedly to increase its power so it could be heard at a longer distance as during transmission much power is lost in term of heat or electric current. A repeater consists of a radio receiver, an amplifier, a transmitter, an isolator, and two antennas. They omit the nuisance during a transmission making signals and sound clear. There are a lot of people around the corner using repeaters as a mean of communication. They carry signals from radios in its surrounding and increase its power to be heard at a longer distance. People who use repeaters are on emergency communication and keep backup power as they use an external source of power.

The internet does have repeaters. All you need is to click repeater option and have to write the address of another person using a repeater and what you will be saying over your radio can be heard on the other side of the hand.

Survival Graffiti

Art can be life-saving in case of a disaster. Only a spray paint can give a clue about the route of the exit of a person or family who can later be rescued. Family members can be taught about different signals or signs distinct to a particular condition and understood by only specific family members. These practices can be made friendly and joyful as well can be fed in memory of every family member if planned as a game adventure. Not only sign and signals can help to trace but also writing text message directly that "I went to that place, or that way" can be used but these direct clues could alert an unknown person who should not get aware of the location.

The most appropriate way are signs and symbols only known by family members should be used. There could be a possible situation when a wife does not reach home on time, and there is no way to contact. Husband can trace her by following her regular or alternate route to the home where a private message in terms of sign or signal can be found and can reunite the couple without wasting time in unavailing search and suffering others.

Emergency Caches

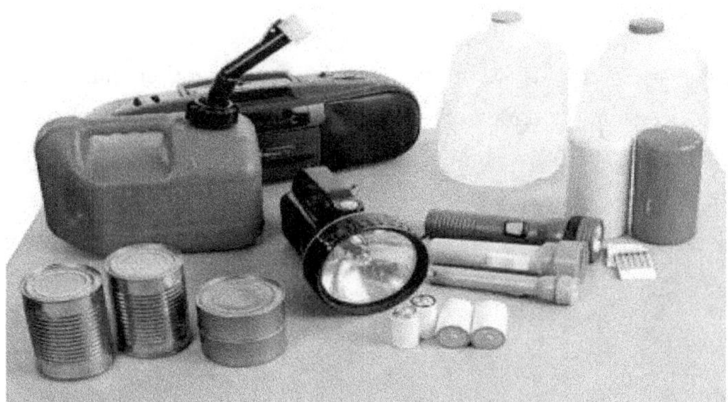

Caches are the substances which are same in type and are stored in unreachable places. Different types of caches can be located at various places only known by family members as trace. These can be placed from school to home or workplace to home at every possible path. These not only provide a trace of the path but also play a role as hidden message and meeting point to reunite. The path of cache needs to skillfully plan out even if it's of short distance covering few miles so that in the case of emergency it can easily be followed.

Hidden messages can be given by placing them in the caches that could be in the form of a pen, paper, painted cans, symbols or simply written message. These messages can serve to re-locate family members, change of plan or meeting point. Any information about personal location can bring about a mental and emotional relief to family members who get separated in any sort of atrocity.

The maps about the track of caches should be placed bags, get me home bags, and especially in the children's backpacks and children should be known to these places and those should be approachable at the time of need.

In case if the caches are being lost or hidden by a delinquent so there should be emergency caches. These emergency caches serve as ultimate approach retrieve communication and uniting family members once they have been separated.

Conclusion

Effective communication truly is one of the best survival skills that you can learn. The very act of being able to get a hold of your relatives to send and receive information will be invaluable and potentially lifesaving.

What you need to do is you need to develop a family emergency communications plan, and you need to confirm that everybody in your family knows the plan (this is why practicing the plan will come in handy).

It's not likely that everyone in your family is going to be together when disaster strikes: your kids could be in school or visiting friends, you could be at work or running errands, and so on.

This is why you must absolutely have a firm plan in place to ensure that everyone in your family can find each other during the emergency situation.

Thank you for purchasing this book; it is my sincere hope that you will apply the required knowledge productively.

www.ingramcontent.com/pod-product-compliance
Lightning Source LLC
Chambersburg PA
CBHW050845260726
48660CB00006B/2454